David Beckham

Revised Edition

By Jeff Savage

AMAZING ATHLETES

Lerner Publications Company • Minneapolis

For Taylor and Bailey—always remember to hustle, be aggressive, and S.I.U.!

Lerner Publications Company
A division of Lerner Publishing Group, Inc.
241 First Avenue North
Minneapolis, MN 55401 U.S.A.

Website address: www.lernerbooks.com

Library of Congress Cataloging-in-Publication Data

Savage, Jeff, 1961–
    David Beckham / by Jeff Savage. — Revised edition.
      pages   cm. — (Amazing athletes)
    Includes index.
    ISBN 978-1-4677-1159-3 (lib. bdg. : alk. paper)
    1. Beckham, David, 1975––Juvenile literature. 2. Soccer players—England—Biography—Juvenile literature. I. Title.
  GV942.7.B432S28 2013
  796.334092—dc23 [B]   2012030080

Manufactured in the United States of America
1 – DP – 12/31/12

TABLE OF CONTENTS

David *(left)* controls the ball against the Houston Dynamo.

"As Good as It Gets"

Los Angeles (LA) Galaxy **midfielder** David Beckham stepped back and lined up the soccer ball. He moved forward and swung his right leg. He sent a **corner kick** rocketing to the front of the net. David's teammate Adam Cristman jumped for the ball. But Cristman's **header** sailed wide of the goal.

David and the Galaxy were playing the Houston Dynamo in the 2011 Major League Soccer (MLS) championship game. The winning team would take home the MLS Cup. The score was tied, 0–0. As usual, all eyes were on David.

David wears the number 23 for the LA Galaxy. He said he chose the number to honor basketball legend Michael Jordan, who also wore 23.

Fans cheer during the 2011 MLS championship game.

5

David boots the ball down the field.

He is the most famous soccer player in the world. He is one of the most famous athletes in any sport.

LA had another chance to score on a **possession** near the beginning of the second half. David kicked the ball across the field and over the heads of the Dynamo **defenders**. It was a perfect **crossing pass**.

The ball landed at the feet of Galaxy player Robbie Keane. Keane kicked the ball into the

David is known for his amazing **free kicks**. He can boom the ball nearly 100 miles per hour.

back of the net. But the referee said the goal didn't count. Keane was **offsides**. David and his teammates would have to try again.

The Galaxy had the ball again a few minutes later. David flicked a header to Keane, who passed the ball to teammate Landon Donovan. Donovan knocked the ball into the net as the crowd roared! The Galaxy took the lead, 1–0. David and Keane were credited with **assists** on the goal.

With a one-goal lead, LA focused on defense. They kept the ball away from their net.

Landon Donovan *(left)* and David hug after Donovan scored a goal to take the lead over the Dynamo.

When time ran out, the score was still 1–0. The Galaxy had won the MLS Cup!

David celebrated with his teammates on the field. He gave Donovan a big hug for scoring the winning goal. David waved to his wife, Victoria, and their children in the stands. It was a big victory for the world's biggest soccer star.

"This guy is as good as it gets," said Galaxy coach Bruce Arena of David after winning the MLS Cup. "He has an unbelievable desire to win. And he's done it all now."

David holds the MLS Cup while celebrating the Galaxy's big win.

David's parents, Ted and Sandra Beckham, are both soccer fans.

MAKING GOALS

David Robert Joseph Beckham was born May 2, 1975, in London, England. He grew up in the nearby town of Chingford. His father, David "Ted" Beckham, worked as a plumber. His mother, Sandra, was a hairdresser. David has two sisters, Lynne and Joanne.

David was a shy, well-behaved boy. His favorite subject in elementary school was art. He also enjoyed sports, such as basketball, rugby, and long-distance running. His favorite sport was soccer, which is called football in Europe.

The Beckhams were big fans of the popular Manchester United Football Club. They often traveled together to see the team play. Like millions of other British boys, David dreamed of playing for the great Man U team.

When he was eight years old, David joined a local youth soccer team. His coach and his father helped him learn the arts

Manchester United is one of the most famous sports teams in the world. The team has more than 50 million fans and 200 official fan clubs.

The Man U team *(shown here in a 1982 game)* are called the Red Devils for their red shirts.

of dribbling, passing, and shooting. David developed excellent footwork and a gift for keeping the ball away from defenders.

David was 11 years old when he came off the field one day after a game. "It's good that you played well today," his mother told him, "because Manchester United were watching you, and they want you to come down and have a trial." David looked up at his mother with wide eyes. He began crying with joy.

The trial was a soccer skills tournament. The most talented boys in England showed off their skills to a panel of judges. David won the event with the highest score ever! His reward was a trip to a soccer camp.

Over the next few years, David continued to improve his game. Pro teams kept an eye on his progress. Then, on July 8, 1991, David's dream came true. Manchester United offered him a **contract**. At just 16 years old, he joined the club as a **trainee**.

Manchester U's youth team *(above)* parades with their 1992 Football Association Youth Cup trophy at the 1993 finals.

STARDOM

David spent the next few years developing his skills on Man U's youth team. Near the end of the 1994–1995 season, David was called up to the **English Premier League (EPL)** team. He was just 19 years old, but he had reached the top level of his sport.

The top English teams compete for three different titles each season. The English Premier League title goes to the team with the league's best regular-season record. The **FA Cup** is a playoff-style tournament between English teams. The **European Cup** is a playoff-style tournament that includes the best clubs from all of Europe.

The following season, David was named a starting midfielder. This meant he needed to cover both ends of the field. The position was a good match for David's cross-country running experience. He ran tirelessly up and down the field. After Man U lost its first game, the team won its next five matches. Man U surprised the soccer world by going on to win the Premier League title and the FA Cup.

In the first game of the 1996–1997 season, David gained fame on an amazing play. Toward the end of a match against Wimbledon, David took the ball at midfield. He noticed Wimbledon goalkeeper Neil Sullivan was standing far out from the net. David drilled a high, booming kick from 60 yards away. The ball sailed over everyone and curled into the net for a goal!

David celebrates his incredible goal against Wimbledon. Man U went on to win the game 3–0.

David's spectacular play made the front page of British newspapers. It was the talk of the soccer world. The victory started Man U on a 15-game unbeaten streak. The team won its second league title in a row. David was voted the Premiership's Young Player of the Year.

The following spring, David saw a music video of the popular musical group, the Spice Girls. One of the girls, Posh Spice, caught his eye. Her real name was Victoria Adams, and the two soon met in person. They began dating.

Victoria Adams and David Beckham

On the field, David enjoyed a huge 1997–1998 season. He scored a career-best nine goals for Man U. After matches, he signed autographs for fans and posed for photographers. Companies such as Gillette, Adidas, and Coca-Cola paid him millions to promote their products. He was a superstar.

Thousands of fans traveled to France to see David play for England in the 1998 World Cup.

OVERCOMING DISASTER

Every four years, billions of soccer fans follow the FIFA (Federation Internationale de Football Association) World Cup. Teams from 32 countries compete in the monthlong World Cup finals tournament. National pride is at stake. Fans are desperate to see their national teams do well. Players feel a ton of pressure.

In 1998, David was a member of England's team. He was just 23. His manager wasn't sure David could handle the pressure. But England was struggling. David was just too good to keep on the bench. His brilliant passing and a great free kick helped England win two key games. David became a national hero.

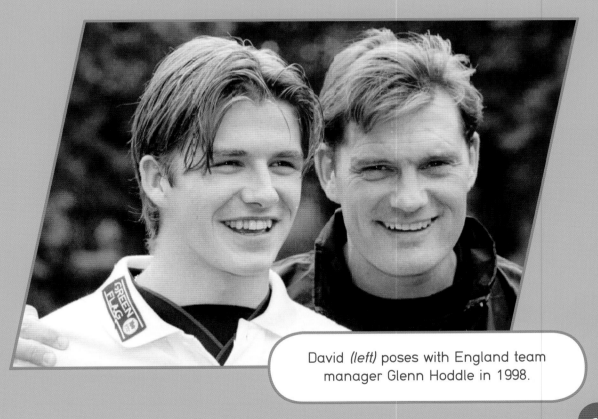

David *(left)* poses with England team manager Glenn Hoddle in 1998.

Then disaster struck! David lost his cool in a close game against Argentina. With the match tied 2–2, Argentine player Diego Simeone knocked David to the ground. David was furious. He reacted by kicking at Simeone.

The referee saw David's kick and gave him a **red card**. David was "sent off"—thrown out of the game. Worse yet, England had to finish the match one man short. They ended up losing. Millions of fans blamed David. Newspaper headlines called him "stupid," "idiot," and other

David *(right)* looks at the referee after Argentina's Diego Simeone knocks him down. David expected Simeone to get the penalty.

David *(second from left)* looks on in disbelief as the referee shows the red card.

insults. He even received death threats. No one felt worse than David.

The booing didn't stop when the 1998–1999 Man U season started. "It was hard concentrating," David admitted. But after a while, the booing just made him play harder.

David helped lead Man U to a historic season. His superb crossing passes produced many goals. "He is the best passer of a ball in the world," said star Ryan Giggs.

Man U became the first English team to win all three titles—the Premier League, FA Cup, and European Cup—in the same season! David's play had won over the fans again.

He had also won over Posh Spice. On July 4, 1999, David and Victoria were married at a castle. Posh and Becks moved into a big mansion. News photographers and TV cameras followed them everywhere. English soccer fans wanted to be just like David. When he changed his hairstyle, thousands of fans did the same.

David and teammate Teddy Sheringham *(right)* celebrate winning the 1999 European Cup.

David *(left)* accepts the red captain's armband from England coach Peter Taylor in 2000.

CAPTAIN AMERICA

David helped Man U win four Premiere League titles. He was captain of both Man U and England's World Cup team. He signed a new contract with Man U that made him the highest-paid soccer player in the world.

English fans had high hopes for the 2002 World Cup finals. But top-ranked Brazil dashed England's dreams with a hard-fought win.

Soon after the World Cup, Man U sold David's contract to Spanish club Real Madrid. Man U received $41 million to let David go.

For the next four years, David dazzled Spanish fans with his magical passing and shot making. He remained captain of England's national team for the 2006 World Cup. The team played well but lost to Portugal.

Rumors began to spread about David playing in the United States. The dreams of millions of U.S. soccer fans came true in January 2007.

David (center) shows off his new Los Angeles Galaxy jersey.

David Beckham, soccer's greatest superstar, announced he would join the LA Galaxy. The team quickly named him captain.

More than 27,000 fans packed the Home Depot Center near Los Angeles in July 2007 to see David's first game with the Galaxy. When David took the field, the crowd roared. Camera flashes lit up the stadium.

The Galaxy lost David's first game with the team, 1–0. But the fans in the stands had seen soccer history. "The reaction to me was incredible," David said.

David *(left)* nurses a knee injury on the Galaxy bench next to assistant coach Trevor James.

David's arrival in LA brought a lot of attention to the team. But the Galaxy didn't play well on the field, and David was often injured. They missed the playoffs in both 2007 and 2008.

The team turned things around in 2009. LA made it all the way to the MLS championship game against Real Salt Lake. The score was tied 1–1 when time ran out, so the game was decided by a **shootout**. David scored his shootout chance, but his team came up short.

David seriously injured his **Achilles tendon**

early in 2010. He had surgery and missed all of the 2010 MLS season. David also could not play for his home country in the 2010 World Cup.

David healed in time for his finest MLS season so far. He scored 2 goals and 15 assists in 2011. Even better, David led his team to victory in the MLS championship game.

David was off to another strong start in 2012. He scored seven goals and nine assists through his team's first 21 games. But a bigger thrill awaited.

David keeps his eyes on the ball during a Galaxy game in 2012.

Fans were thrilled to see David pilot the speedboat with the Olympic torch on board.

London, where David was born, hosted the 2012 Summer Olympics. David steered the speedboat that brought the Olympic torch into the stadium.

Victoria Beckham also took part in the Olympic ceremonies. She performed with her old band, the Spice Girls.

David has become one of the most successful athletes in the world. But as a child, he never dreamed of being famous. "All I ever wanted to do was kick a football about," he said.

Selected Career Highlights

2012 Had second most assists (nine) on Galaxy through first 21 games

2011 Led Galaxy in assists (15)
Led Galaxy to MLS Cup victory

2010 Missed entire season with injury

2009 Scored two goals and three assists in just 11 games

2008 Led Galaxy in assists (10)

2007 Joined Major League Soccer as a member of the Los Angeles Galaxy
Led Real Madrid to the Spanish league title

2006 Became the first English player in World Cup history to score a goal in three World Cup tournaments
Led the Spanish League in assists

2003 Joined the Real Madrid team

2002 Scored the winning goal to defeat Argentina in the World Cup match

2001 Runner-up for the FIFA World Player of the Year
Scored the tying goal versus Greece to qualify England for the World Cup
Led Manchester United to the FA Premier League championship

2000 Led Manchester United to the FA Premier League championship

1999 Runner-up for FIFA World Player of the Year
Runner-up for the European Footballer of the Year
Led Manchester United to the European Cup title
Led Manchester United to the English FA Cup title
Led Manchester United to the FA Premier League championship

1998 Led England to the qualifying win for the World Cup

1997 Named Professional Footballers' Association Young Player of the Year
Led Manchester United to the FA Premier League championship

1996 Led Manchester United to the English FA Cup title
Led Manchester United to FA Premier League championship

Glossary

Achilles tendon: a tough cord that connects the lower back leg muscles to the heel

assists: passes to teammates that help score goals

contract: an agreement signed between a player and a team

corner kick: a direct free kick taken from the corner area after the ball is played out of bounds past the goal line by the defending team

crossing pass: a pass from one side of the field to the other

defenders: players whose job it is to try to stop the other team from scoring

English Premier League (EPL): the top league of English soccer teams. The team with the best record in Premier League play wins the Premier League title

European Cup: a yearly tournament held to decide the best team in Europe. Officially known as the Union of European Football Associations (UEFA) Champions League.

FA Cup: a yearly tournament in which professional English soccer teams compete to decide the country's top team. Officially called the Football Association Challenge Cup.

free kicks: special kicks awarded to teams when opponents commit penalties

header: hitting the ball in the air with your head

midfielder: a position on a soccer team whose main responsibility is covering the middle of the field

offsides: in soccer, a player is offsides if he or she is closer to the other team's goal than both the ball and the last defender

possession: when a player or a team has control of the ball

red card: a card given out by a referee for unsportsmanlike conduct. A player who is given a red card is sent off from the game, and the team must finish the game one player short.

shootout: in soccer, five players from each team take turns shooting on a goal defended by a goalie

trainee: a new player who learns the team's rules and plays

Further Reading & Websites

Eason, Sarah, and Paul Mason. *Street Soccer*. Minneapolis: Lerner Publications Company, 2012.

Pendleton, Ken. *David Beckham*. Minneapolis: Twenty-First Century Books, 2007.

Robinson, Tom. *David Beckham: Soccer's Superstar*. Berkeley Heights, NJ: Enslow Publishers, 2008.

Los Angeles Galaxy: The Official Site
http://la.galaxy.mlsnet.com
The official website of the Los Angeles Galaxy includes the team schedule and game results, late-breaking news, biographies of David Beckham, and much more.

Manchester United: The Official Site
http://www.manutd.com
Manchester United's official website features news and game schedules, video highlights, player profiles, and history.

Sports Illustrated Kids
http://www.sikids.com
The *Sports Illustrated Kids* website covers all sports, including soccer.

Index

Photo Acknowledgments

The images in this book are used with the permission of: © Jeff Gross/
Getty Images, p. 4; © Icon SMI, p. 5; © Matthew Ashton/AMA/CORBIS, p. 6;
© Andy Mead/YCJ/Icon SMI, p. 7; © Toby Canham/Stringer/Getty Images,
p. 8; © Mike Egerton/EMPICS Sports/PA Photos, p. 9; © Mike Brett/PA Photos,
p. 11; © Laurence Griffiths/EMPICS Sport/PA Photos, p. 13; © Michael
Cooper/Getty Images, p. 15; © Chris Sunerland/Stringer/Reuters/CORBIS,
p. 16; © Trinity Mirror/MirrorPix/Alamy, p. 18; © Adam Butler/PA Archive/
PA Photos, p. 19; © Gerald Cerles/AFP/Getty Images, p. 20; © Offside Sports
Photography/Alamy, p. 21; © Glyn Kirk/Action Plus/Icon SMI, p. 22; © Owen
Humphreys/PA Archive/PA Photos, p. 23; AP Photo/Kevork Djansezian,
pp. 24, 26; © Nick Laham/Getty Images, p. 25; © John Hefti/Icon SMI,
p. 27; © KMSP/DPPI/Icon SMI, p. 28; © Victor Decolongon/Stringer/Getty
Images, p. 29.

Front cover: © Bob Levey/Stringer/Getty Images.

Main body text set in Caecilia LT Std 55 Roman 16/28.
Typeface provided by Adobe Systems.